GREAT EXPLORATIONS

CAPTAIN JAMES COOK

Three Times Around the World

MILTON MELTZER

BENCHMARK BOOKS

MARSHALL CAVENDISH
NEW YORK

With special thanks to Professor David Armitage, Columbia University
for his careful reading of this manuscript.

Benchmark Books
Marshall Cavendish Corporation
99 White Plains Road
Tarrytown, New York 10591-9001

Library of Congress Cataloging-in-Publication Data
Meltzer, Milton, date
Captain James Cook: Three Times Around the World / by Milton Meltzer
p. cm. – (Great explorations)
Includes bibliographical references and index.
ISBN 0-7614-1240-9
1. Cook, James, 1728-1779—Journeys—Juvenile literature. 2. Explorers—Great Britain—Biography—
Juvenile literature. 3. Voyages around the world—Juvenile literature. [1. Cook, James, 1728-1779.
2. Explorers. 3. Voyages around the world.] I. Title. II. Series.
G420.C65 M45 2001 910'.92—dc21 [B] 00-051899

Photo Research by Candlepants Incorporated
Cover Photo: Giraudon / Art Resource, NY. Inset: Bettmann / Corbis
The photographs in this book are used by permission and through the courtesy of; *CORBIS:* 14, 68, 72; Bettmann,
4, 17, 23, 31; Douglas Peebles, 8; Archivo Iconografico, S.A., 20; Robert Garvey, 25; Gianni Dagli Orti, 33;
Wolfgang Kaehler, 51; Mike Zens, 62. *The Art Archive* : 6, 13, 29, 37, 41, 45, 47, 48, 55, 59, 63, 65, 70. *Art Resource,
NY* : Alinari, 10; Scala, 12; SEF, 19; Werner Forman Archive, National Museum of new Zealand, Wellington, 39.
Beinecke Rare Book and Manuscript Library / Yale University : 58.

Printed in Hong Kong
1   3   5   6   4   2

Contents

Foreword 5

ONE An Apprentice at Sea 7

TWO Master of a Warship 16

THREE A Southern Continent? 22

FOUR Time in Tahiti 28

FIVE The Maori of New Zealand 36

SIX Australia: A New Continent 44

SEVEN Into the Antarctic 50

EIGHT A Northwest Passage? 57

NINE We Had Lost a Father 67

Captain Cook and His Times 75

Further Research 76

Bibliography 77

Index 79

Captain James Cook landing in the New Hebrides.

foreword

Whether young in age or young in heart, who doesn't dream of doing something extraordinary? Discovering a cure for cancer? Finding a buried treasure? Painting a beautiful picture, or writing a magnificent poem that people will enjoy hundreds of years from now?

This is the story of a man who came from nowhere and made a mark on the world never to be forgotten. James Cook was one of the greatest explorer-seamen the world has ever known. Few men have done more to alter and correct the map of the earth. Three times during the eighteenth century, Cook's ships sailed across the world's oceans. His crews knew delight and despair, the burning heat of the tropics and the freezing cold of the polar regions. They were faced with both intimate and hostile encounters with foreign people, storms, shipwrecks, hunger, and death. Captain Cook, said one historian, "covered more sea distance, discovered more new lands and contributed more to the sum of human knowledge than any explorer of his time."

Amid the icebergs of the continent of Antartica.

This book will try to tell you something of the world that shaped Captain Cook and the personal qualities that made his achievements possible.

*   *   *

Sometimes the best way to convey the thoughts and feelings of Captain Cook and the men under his command will be through extracts from their journals. For easier reading I have taken some liberty in modernizing language, spelling, and punctuation. Yet without, I hope, changing the meaning.

ONE

An Apprentice at Sea

It was a chilly time of year when he came into the world. "James, ye son of a day labourer," reads the baptismal record in the village church of Marton. His birth date was October 27, 1728.

The infant's father, a Scot who had moved south to the Yorkshire district of England in search of work, was also named James Cook. With no training for a trade, he settled into farm labor and married Grace Pace, a local girl. They lived in a two-room clay thatched-roofed cottage, where James junior was born. The couple had six other children, four of whom died before the age of five.

When James was six or seven, a Mrs. Walker, whose husband was a prosperous farmer, began to teach the boy the alphabet and how to read and write. In exchange for the lessons, James tended the stock, watered the horses, and ran errands for the Walker family.

The Cook family cottage where the explorer was born. Much later it was moved from Yorkshire to Australia, whose east coast Cook was the first to chart.

Two years later, his family moved to the larger village of Ayton nearby, where Mr. Cook had been made a farm manager. The owner of the farm, noting that little James was bright, paid the fees for him to attend the local school. There he continued to improve his reading and writing. He showed an aptitude for arithmetic but had some trouble with spelling. According to a village historian, he showed no brilliance in his schoolwork, but "he had an obstinate and sturdy way of his own . . . something in his manners and deportment" that earned the respect of the other boys.

That James had this much schooling was unusual. Except for a small number of the middle and upper classes, few could read or write in that time.

When James was seventeen, his father learned that William Sanderson, a grocer and draper in the seaside town of Staithes, needed a helper. Mr. Sanderson took the boy on as an apprentice. He weighed out biscuits and bacon and poultry and measured ribbons while sneaking looks out the windows at the bustling life of the harbor on the North Sea. Boats were always coming and going, and the tangy odors of seaweed and fish teased his nostrils every time the door opened.

Though James did his job well, he soon knew that the life of a shopkeeper was not for him. Yet he stayed on for a year and a half. Mr. Sanderson must have sensed his unhappiness in the retail trade, for he took a step that would change James's life forever. He brought the boy some twenty miles off to meet a friend, James Walker, a shipmaster in the much larger town of Whitby. Out of that seaport hundreds of ships sailed to the Baltic, the Mediterranean, even to America, India, and China.

Mr. Walker owned several ships engaged in the coal trade. Man and boy hit it off at once. James signed on for a three-year apprenticeship and was given lodging in Walker's home. To eighteen-year-old James, who had never been anyplace but a village, Whitby was a grand city. Its ten thousand inhabitants worked as fishermen, in the sail-makers' lofts, or making rope and cordage for shipbuilders. Far more crewed the more than two hundred ships the port boasted. This was industry and enterprise on a scale that dazzled the country boy.

The Walkers were Quakers, respected for their honesty and decency. Quakers believed in an inner spiritual light that inspired them to be helpful to others. So when James was offered food and lodging in the Walker home, he came under the best influence. Mr. Walker prized learning and encouraged the boy to improve his mathematics, to study books on astronomy and the theory of navigation, to learn how to use the compass and figure out latitude and longitude (as best one could at this time), to read sailing charts and understand the design of ships.

James's practical learning came on Walker's ships. The industrial revolution was about to take off in Britain and Europe, and coal would be needed to fuel the factories as they opened up. Ships built for the purpose, called colliers, carried coal from port to port—a million tons a year. Walker's company shipped coal from the mines of northeastern England to London, the Netherlands, Norway, and other Baltic ports.

One of the busy seaports Cook sailed to during his apprenticeship in the coal trade.

An Apprentice at Sea

Young Cook began his life at sea in February 1747 on a typical collier—three-masted, square-rigged, some four hundred tons, about one hundred feet (thirty meters) in length and twenty-seven (eight meters) in beam. On his first voyage the crew numbered nineteen—a master, mate, carpenter, and cook, five seamen, and ten apprentices aged fifteen to nineteen. Such coastal voyages might run for a month or two or more.

Sailing England's east coast was a tough schooling in seamanship, for it was treacherous, without lights, without buoys. The charts that pilots used for guidance were roughly done. The ships risked hitting sunken rocks and rocky shelves, breakers, sandpits, and sandbanks. Weather could be foggy or stormy. Every seaman knew of, and never forgot, times when ships were wrecked and all hands died. Once when sixteen ships sailed out together, only six returned. And who could forget the day when twenty-three ships went down in a terrible storm off the Norfolk coast?

To be a young apprentice was to take on a man's work, hard work. You had to learn your ship and everything about it, from how it was put together and how to sail it to how to repair it when damaged. Master, mate, and seamen were your models. If they were capable and strict instructors, you were lucky. You were assigned all kinds of tasks, from the simplest to the most difficult and dangerous. If you were lazy or clumsy you were given the scut work—cleaning jobs—until you proved you could do better. It was a point of honor to do your job and do it right.

As J. C. Beaglehole, a Cook biographer, put it: "To handle a ship, not merely in a gale at sea, but in the narrow entrance of a small river harbour, or over the shifting sand-banks of the Thames, with other shipping about, to keep her off the bottom or know when she could safely rest upon it, to bring her to anchor or get her under weigh in a crowd, these might be feats of learning or technique indeed."

Apprentices usually got a half-day's shore leave per week. If they

In Cook's time, shipwreck by storm was every seaman's greatest fear.

were unloading at a wharf on the Thames, they got leave to go up to London and see the sights. At that time the city's population was about half a million. (In all England there were some six million people.)

It was a squalid city, the streets unpaved and narrow, and with no sanitary system, it stank. The contrast between the luxury of the rich and the poverty of the mass of Londoners was glaring. The poor lived in desperately overcrowded one- or two-room hovels. Disease was rampant and death routine. Still, people from the country migrated to the city in an endless stream. Apart from craftsmen and journeymen, most city folk were laborers, who had only their muscle and sweat to

The city of London must have been quite an impressive sight to young James Cook. In fact, the city was a dirty, crowded place.

offer. They never enjoyed steady jobs and depended on casual work. Unions were forbidden by law, so workers could be dismissed at will, plunging them into abject poverty. The poor and propertyless had no political rights, and as yet only a few thinking people believed they *should* have them.

Sir Francis Drake, the Elizabethan admiral who sailed around the world from 1577 to 1580.

If you chose to go to sea to make a living, you got miserable pay, unending hours, long stretches of time away from home and family. The ship's master was your lord, his word the *final* word.

Yet thousands and thousands of men chose the sea. For James Cook, maybe it was the prospect of life in a dismal village selling cheese and ribbons that led to his choice.

When young Cook showed promise, Walker promoted him quickly. In 1748 Walker was fitting out a large collier. Cook was told to pitch in, learning much about ship design and construction that would benefit him later. Then he joined the new coal ship's crew.

In April 1750 Cook's three-year apprenticeship was over. A full-fledged seaman now, he was confident he could handle any of Walker's ships. At the end of 1752 he passed the examination for a mate's rating. Three years later, Walker offered to upgrade him to master of a ship.

But Cook said no. At twenty-seven, he had served for nine years in the North Sea, the Irish Sea, the Baltic Sea, and the English Channel. He wanted to travel beyond those horizons. He had read of the great English seafarers such as Hawkins and Drake, as well as of the exploits of the Dutch, the Spanish, and the Portuguese. Why couldn't he see the worlds they had discovered? And perhaps someday find new worlds himself?

So he joined the Royal Navy.

T W O

Master of a Warship

A beginner in the navy? At twenty-seven? To the other sailors he looked like an old man. Most of them had enlisted in their early teens. Some parents enrolled sons as young as eight. In wartime many sailors never volunteered at all; they were snatched out of waterfront hangouts or off the street and forced to serve.

Why would a man who had risen to master of a merchant ship sign on to the hardships of the navy? The pay was poor, the food worse, the discipline harsh. For wrongdoing you could be flogged or shot or hanged. If you escaped drowning and the enemy didn't kill you, you would likely die of scurvy or typhus.

Perhaps Cook was smarter than it would appear. This was 1755 and Britain was getting ready for still another war with France, her great rival for empire. This time the conflict was over control of colonies

James Cook,
in his naval uniform.

in America. Would someone with Cook's experience, his skills, have a chance to rise in the navy? Most unlikely, for he was a commoner, and upper-class snobbery made it very hard for such a man to gain any position of authority.

But Cook had great self-confidence, even this early. He felt sure that in wartime he would rise rapidly. He proved to be right. In a month he was promoted to master's mate.

In 1756 war broke out. The Europeans called it the Seven Years' War; the Americans, the French and Indian War. Cook served on a ship under Captain Hugh Palliser, another Yorkshire man. He spotted Cook's special qualities early on and acted as his mentor. He taught Cook trigonometry and deepened his skills in navigation and charting. Later Palliser would be of great help to Cook.

Their ship kept close to the English coast, patrolling for enemy vessels. Cook's first time under enemy fire came in a battle with a big fifty-gun French warship. Maimings and mutilation: a head blown away, a leg sliced off, a gut ripped out. . . The British suffered ten dead and eighty wounded, while the French losses were fifty killed and thirty wounded. Cook's courage was tested in combat and found solid. He came through unharmed, and the French ship was taken over.

In October 1757, after only two years in service, the navy made Cook master of a new sixty-four-gun warship in a fleet of eight ships sailing across the Atlantic to seize French colonies in Canada. Here was the long voyage he had yearned for while carrying coal to London. He was keeping a log now, the first of many that help us know what he saw and did and thought. He took part in the capture of two French strongholds, Louisburg in 1758 and Quebec in 1759, which broke the French hold on that part of North America.

In the course of this service Cook became friendly with an army engineer, Samuel Holland, assigned to survey Britain's new-won territory. Cook grasped that Lieutenant Holland's methods and instruments could

This English warship, heavily armed with cannon, resembles the ship Cook commanded during the French and Indian War.

be applied to sea charting, and he asked the engineer to teach him his craft.

Holland enjoyed having an eager and talented pupil, and the two worked together for several months, creating charts of every turn of the coast, every point and cove, every reef and rock. Soon Cook asked his captain's permission to let him work on surveys himself.

Master of a Warship

Until the fall of 1762, Cook was busy charting Canadian rivers, bays, and coasts. Two of his charts were valued highly enough to be printed in London in a book that would be used by generations of seamen.

Senior officers had begun to notice what an extraordinary man Cook was, how skillful and responsible. Lord Colville, under whom Cook had served, wrote the British Admiralty to praise Cook's "genius and capacity" and to recommend him "for greater undertakings."

The Seven Years' War ended in 1763, with France yielding Canada to the British. Cook sailed home. He had been gone over four years, and was now thirty-four. Soon after his return he met twenty-two year-old Elizabeth Batts, and within six weeks they were married.

What did the new bride see in him? A tall, powerful man, with brown eyes and hair, a strong nose and mouth, and lines of maturity on

London celebrates the end of the Seven Years War with a great fireworks display.

his face—a good-looking man, it was said, "in a plain sort of way." A friend noted that he was a lively talker, and by now with the richest experience to draw on. But he was no braggart. Throughout his life Cook would always be modest and sensitive to others.

James and Elizabeth enjoyed only a few months of domestic life before the navy sent him back across the Atlantic to Newfoundland. His task was to map the entire coastline—some six thousand miles (ten thousand kilometers).

Working both from ship and on shore, Cook used what he had learned of land surveying and combined it with marine charting. The outcome was one of the most detailed and accurate sea charts anyone had done up to that time.

The navy set the rhythm for the work: Each spring and summer Cook worked in Newfoundland, charting; each fall and winter he worked back home preparing the charts for publication. During these years his wife bore two boys, James and Nathaniel.

About fifty of Cook's superb charts have been preserved in various collections. Some, as large as ten feet long, are on a scale of one inch to one mile. They include much inland mapping too, showing lakes and rivers, as well as harbors, headlands, and sea depths. As Richard Hough, a biographer of Cook, puts it, for Cook "every mark on the fine hand-made paper was like a satisfactory note to the composer of a great symphony."

During Cook's 1766 expedition his innate curiosity led him to make observations of an eclipse of the sun, which were forwarded to the Royal Society (the Royal Society for Improving Natural Knowledge, founded in 1645) in London, impressing that august body as "very expert." A hundred years later, a scientist working in Newfoundland remarked that the accuracy of Cook's charts was "truly astonishing." No wonder then, when a great new voyage of discovery was being discussed by the Royal Society, the name of James Cook came to mind.

THREE

A Southern Continent?

With his survey work in Newfoundland completed, Cook had more time for his wife and two boys. The frequent separations must have been hard on them all. He saw his friend Captain Palliser and dropped in on the Admiralty people. Those high-ranking veterans of the sea admired this man, who, with almost no formal education, had already contributed significantly to the advancement of navigation and science.

Cook learned that the Royal Society was planning to send an expedition to Tahiti to observe a rare event, the transit of the planet Venus across the face of the sun. It would occur on June 3, 1769. Observations taken from many sites around the earth could provide the basis for astronomers to calculate the distance between the earth and the sun, and thus help scientists to map the solar system.

King George III of England knew that exploration would benefit Britain's economy. This, and not scientific discovery, was his main reason for funding Cook's 1768 expedition.

A Southern Continent?

The British were in a hurry to launch the project because another transit would not occur until 1874. Tahiti had been chosen because there was a good chance that from this island in the South Pacific skies would be clear.

The Royal Society had convinced King George III to provide funding for the expedition. He understood the importance of scientific inquiry and the need for the government to back it. Not just for the sake of science, but because navigation—and therefore commerce—depended on accurate astronomical data.

The navy would provide the ship and the crew. But who would lead the expedition? Someone suggested James Cook. What? Put a noncommissioned officer in command? Could the son of a Yorkshire farm laborer, who had entered the navy as a common seaman, be given such a high post? It seemed impossible in eighteenth-century Britain, where talent and intelligence were believed to be the sole property of the upper class.

But it was precisely Cook's skills at navigation and mapmaking that this task required. So almost by a miracle, Cook was chosen and promoted to lieutenant, a rank befitting his new responsibilities.

Britain was eager to expand its influence in the Pacific, for control of the seas was vital to economic and political power. There were other questions too that needed answers. The Pacific had been crisscrossed often since the time of Ferdinand Magellan two hundred years before. But there were still great blanks on the ocean's map. For centuries, legends of a Great Southern Continent had teased the popular mind. Was it really there? At the foot of the globe? And if it was, what was its size and shape? Who lived there? Could it be developed to a nation's advantage? Britain had already planted colonies in North America and extended its influence in India and in several other parts of the world. After completing the work at Tahiti, Cook's instructions were to map the geography of the Pacific, to plant the British flag on any territory he could claim, and to "proceed southward in order to make discovery of the Continent."

The ship chosen for the expedition was the *Endeavour*, a converted Whitby collier of 368 tons, ninety-seven feet (thirty meters) long, with a twenty-nine-foot (nine meters) beam. Not a racy frigate or a towering warship, but the kind of sturdy coal-carrier Cook had sailed on for years. Just right, he thought, for rounding Cape Horn and meeting tropical storms.

And now the crew: ninety-four men and boys in all, including twenty-one officers and artisans—gunners, carpenters, midshipmen, quartermasters, a surgeon, a cook, a steward, an armorer, a sailmaker— forty able seamen, twelve marines, eight servants.

A replica of Captain Cook's cabin aboard the <u>Endeavour.</u>

SHIPLOAD

For a voyage of at least two years into the unknown, what food and equipment were needed? The navy's suppliers provided the *Endeavour* with huge amounts of bread, flour, wheat, oatmeal, beef and pork (dried and salted to preserve them), suet, raisins, vinegar, oil, sugar, salt, beer and rum, malt, and sauerkraut, and objects to be traded with the natives—such as nails, mirrors, fishhooks, hatchets, beads, scissors, even a few dolls—were also loaded aboard.

Not to forget the scientific instruments! There were telescopes, a quadrant (an angle-measuring device rarely used today), an astronomical clock, a sextant (an instrument for measuring distances, especially altitudes of celestial bodies), a thermometer, a watch, and a portable tentlike observatory to shelter the instruments. Plus Cook's own mathematical and surveying equipment for determining the ship's position and charting whatever lands they might find.

Monthly or annual wages were set for everyone. A liberal allowance to Mrs. Cook was provided, for this and the two voyages to come.

A Southern Continent?

Most of the ship's company were young. Only Cook and a few others were forty or older. They came from all over Britain and some from abroad. Few could read or write. Some would turn out to be unreliable or shady characters. A rough, tough bunch, used to living in cramped quarters, accustomed to brawling, often drunk. The navy issued a daily pint of rum for each man and half a pint for the boys. If you stole the liquor, you were flogged.

Perhaps most surprising to us today is how very young many were: Isaac Manley, twelve; Alex Hood, fourteen; George Vancouver, fifteen; Isaac Smith and Will Howson, sixteen. Dick Pickersgill, nineteen, a talented surveyor and chartmaker, held the high post of master's mate. Think too of able seaman James Burney, who on a later voyage with Cook, at age twenty-one, had already served eleven years in the navy.

Young people often achieved greatness in service with Captain Cook; several moved up to high posts. It was said of Cook that no one ever attracted, held, or produced better sailors.

This voyage and the two to follow had scientific goals as well as political ones, and Cook was the first to carry a full complement of scientists. Aboard ship were astronomers to record the transit of Venus and the location of landfalls, naturalists to study plant and animal life, and artists to draw or paint native inhabitants and the physical features of land and sea. Several of them were journal keepers who observed the customs of the peoples encountered, thus contributing to the young science of anthropology.

Cook was the only explorer of his century to lead more than one mission to the Pacific. In a ten-year period he would command three voyages, each time building upon what he had learned before, often carrying some of the same officers and men. His voyages would become a model for generations of explorers to come.

F O U R

Time in Tahiti

On August 26, 1768, the *Endeavour* set sail from England. Almost at once a ferocious gale blew up, sickening the civilians aboard. Two of them, Sir Joseph Banks and Dr. Daniel Solander, both naturalists, nevertheless started making notes at once on the sea life they observed, while Sidney Parkinson, an artist, managed to draw a tiny sea insect they had netted.

In ten days they reached the Portuguese island of Madeira, where an anchor slipped away. Trying to retrieve it, the quartermaster became entangled with the rope and anchor, was pulled overboard, and drowned. Banks and Solander went ashore often to collect wild plants and shrubs, finding nearly 700 species. Some crewmen loaded more supplies—poultry, wine, beef, ten tons of fresh water—while others caulked and painted the ship and repaired storm-damaged sails and rigging.

A caricaturist pokes fun at Sir Joseph Banks, the naturalist aboard Captain Cook's ship the <u>Endeavor</u> by turning him into a fantastic creature—a giant caterpillar transforming into an elegant butterfly.

VICTORY OVER SCURVY

Shipwreck was a strong possibility sailors faced in those days. If that disaster didn't kill you, scurvy might. When Cook sailed the Atlantic to fight the French in America, he saw for the first time the appalling effect of a poor diet on long voyages: twenty-six men died of scurvy. It is caused by a vitamin C deficiency, a lack of fresh fruits and vegetables. Teeth fall out, capillaries bleed, the skin blotches, the legs totter, and a person sinks into a lethargy that often ends in death. Merchant mariners and the navy of the time accepted it, even though they lost hundreds of ships and thousands of men to it.

Years before, a Scottish naval surgeon, James Lind, had successfully treated scurvy-ridden sailors with oranges and lemons, both rich in vitamin C. But somehow the Admiralty had ignored his discovery. On his own, Cook decided to fight off scurvy when he took command of the *Endeavour*. He would run a healthy ship by making the crew eat a diet he hoped would defeat scurvy. Somewhere he had

Then on to Brazil. As they crossed the equator, the traditional ceremony was held: If this was your first crossing, you were dunked three times into the sea or forfeited four days' ration of rum—which was divided among the seasoned crew. By nightfall few sober men were aboard.

At Rio de Janeiro another tragedy occurred. A sailor fell from the rigging and drowned before he could be reached.

heard that citrus fruits and leafy vegetables might prevent the illness. Wherever he sailed on his three voyages of discovery, he would test new fruits and grasses on the crew, whether they liked it or not. He enforced cleanliness on board, inspecting the men and their quarters daily and punishing offenders by cutting off their daily grog.

Proof that it worked? On that first voyage he lost not a single man to scurvy. And the record of the following ones was just as impressive. To indicate how important Cook's pioneering fight against scurvy was, note this figure: Dr. Francis E. Cuppage, pathologist and medical historian, estimates that three million sailors worldwide died of scurvy between 1500 and 1800.

A botanical drawing of lemons, which were, like other citrus fruits, vital to the prevention of scurvy.

As they sailed south the temperature fell, and storms rocked the ship. But its tubby design proved secure. Just before Christmas, Banks shot an albatross, but no bad luck (believed to result from killing an albatross) followed, for Christmas day dawned beautifully clear and bright. On New Year's Day they were off the coast of Patagonia, where they saw their first penguins. Then on to the islands Magellan had named Tierra del Fuego—Land of Fire. On January 15, 1769, they stepped ashore to encounter some Fuegian men wearing only loose cloaks over their shoulders despite the cold. (Cook did not know of the seal oil with which they covered their skin from birth to death, allowing them to survive the harsh climate.) The men painted their faces with black lines and wore strings of shells or bones. Their weapons were well-made bows and arrows. Banks, gathering specimens in the interior, came across a settlement of about fifty conical huts, with only a few boughs and a little grass covering the weather side. No furniture, no eating or cooking utensils. It was Cook's first meeting with primitive people. He thought theirs was a "miserable" life.

On what started as a mild clear day, Banks led some ten men into the interior to see what they could find. Suddenly the temperature dropped steeply and snow began to fall. They were forced to spend the night in the forest. All they had to eat was a vulture they shot, skinned, and cooked. At dawn they found two of their group had frozen to death.

Ten days later, the *Endeavour* rounded Cape Horn and entered the Pacific. For some eight weeks they sailed northwesterly over empty seas. Early in March the temperature rose and they shed winter clothing. On April 11 they anchored at Tahiti. Cook had reached his first goal seven weeks before the transit of Venus would occur.

One of the most beautiful Pacific islands, Tahiti rises from hilly slopes to a volcanic peak of seven thousand feet (2,134 meters). A narrow border of fertile land runs around the mountainous mass. Cook was now in the geographic center of Polynesia.

During his voyages over the next ten years he would see how the Polynesian people had spread by canoe over the Pacific and would note the differences among their various branches. He came with preconceived ideas about "primitive" people—their cultures, their political organization, their economies. Although the language barrier was great, he managed to reach some understanding. He and others in the crew piled up valuable notes on houses, weapons, domestic objects, physical characteristics, manners, gestures, emotion—whatever the eye and ear could take in. Their journals would become the starting point for anthropological research in the Pacific. Though often puzzled by what they observed, the visitors were sympathetic.

Cook journeyed around the entire island to chart it accurately. Banks and Solander ranged everywhere in search of plant and animal specimens. The island abounded in rats, which Banks shot and cooked, finding them "good eating."

Parkinson made pen-and-ink drawings of people, canoes, dwellings, and landscapes, adding notes on manners and customs he observed. Invited to dine with chiefs, Cook's staff found that the men

A print depicts Cook and his men sharing a meal with Tahitians.

and women ate separately, although wives sat beside their husbands, feeding them mouthful after mouthful.

When the time came, the observation of the transit of Venus was made. But a hazy glow surrounding the planet made accuracy difficult. And an unforeseen optical distortion spoiled the coordinated readings of the transit made in other parts of the world. Thus no calculation of the distance between the earth and the sun was obtained from this transit. A scientific failure, but not Cook's fault.

As the weeks passed, many of the ship's company took "temporary wives" among the Tahitians. What was considered a sin in Europe was only "a simply innocent gratification" here, Parkinson noted. The prospect of venereal disease had worried Cook terribly, even before they landed at Tahiti. He knew he would be unable to prevent sexual encounters between his men and the Tahitian women, so he had the

SHIPS BEARING DISEASE

Cook's ships brought syphilis, tuberculosis, and an influenza virus to Hawaii. (Some of Cook's men had been tubercular for a long time and would die of the disease before the voyage ended.) Later other Europeans visiting the islands would also introduce diseases unknown before their arrival. The effects were disastrous. The pre-European population of the islands was an estimated 800,000. By 1890, about one hundred years after Cook's visit to Hawaii, barely 40,000 people were left.

ship's surgeon check all the men for symptoms. Only one man had them; he was kept aboard ship. But Cook's precautions didn't help, for signs of disease were already evident among the islanders. Soon a third of the crew were infected too. The Tahitians said that French ships had preceded the English years before and blamed the disease on them. Whoever was responsible, it no longer mattered. Cook predicted that venereal disease "may in time spread itself over all the islands in the South Seas, to the eternal reproach of those who first brought it among them."

The great majority of the Tahitians were commoners—fishermen, laborers, servants of the upper class, craftsmen, artists who tattooed bodies. They and the chiefs eagerly offered provisions to the Europeans, trading especially for nails and edged tools. In all such connections Cook's firm rule for his men was "to endeavor by every fair means to cultivate friendship with the natives and to treat them with all imaginable humanity."

While the British learned something of the complex Tahitian culture, the islanders tried to understand their visitors. But misunderstandings were inevitable. Especially about property. The Tahitians respected their own property rights but not the property rights of the visitors. They swiped all sorts of things, useful or not, partly as a game to show what they could get away with. Not understanding this, Cook sometimes reacted harshly, with punishments out of proportion. Cook's people also showed disrespect for island customs and religious beliefs without realizing it, and so angered the Tahitians.

In mid-July, 1769, after three months in this sailor's paradise, Cook decided to move out. With him went Tupaia, a Tahitian priest, who wanted to visit England. He would be a helpful guide and interpreter as they sailed in search of other islands in the Pacific.

FIVE
The Maori of New Zealand

Within a day at sea Tupaia had guided Cook to a group of small islands he would add to his Pacific chart. Greeted by friendly people, Cook named their home the Society Islands and claimed it for England. He kept heading south, in search of that Great Southern Continent. After several dull weeks in the open seas a lookout spotted a large mountainous land mass. The Southern Continent? Not yet. This was New Zealand, which had first been reached more than a century before by a Dutch explorer who mistakenly thought he had found the Southern Continent.

For the next six months Cook would explore much of the coast, charting it in great detail. The study of its people proved far more difficult. The visitors were not welcome. The Maori people lived in many small tribes, and often fought with their neighbors. Were these

A Maori with tattooed face, drawn by Sydney Parkinson,
an artist who sailed with Cook.

newcomers hostile too? Cook's attempts to establish trade and friendly relations met with rock throwing. In return, shots were fired and several Maori were killed. Cook was deeply upset. Only after he had captured three boys and treated them very well aboard ship did hostility end. Then the Maori even touched noses with the visitors when they met. With this gentle pressure, peace, friendship, and hospitality were offered. The breath of life was shared.

Cook sailed north along the coast, stopping here and there to trade cloth, beads, and nails for fresh water, fish, sweet potatoes, wild celery, and curiosities.

The visitors found that the Maori cultivated their land with great care and skill. Their houses were solid and neat, the rooms clean and well kept. They had outhouses too, a convenience Cook had not seen before in the Pacific.

The men were tattooed in intricate spiral patterns. The women applied thick red paint to their faces. As trust grew, the Maori let the strangers into their homes, answering questions about their beliefs and way of life.

The New Zealanders were masterful at carving, a craft with which they ornamented their houses, boats, and especially their enormous canoes. Banks measured one canoe at over sixty-eight feet (twenty-one meters) long, five feet wide (one-and-a-half meters), and three-and-a-half feet (one meter) deep. The carvings were not realistic, but symbolic—stylized images of men, birds, and fish elaborated with abstract patterns.

Cook learned that the Maori practiced cannibalism, but only of enemies captured in war. Because wars were so frequent they built fortified villages with ditches and palisades. Their weapons consisted of well-made lances, clubs, and darts, but not bows and arrows.

At one anchorage, Banks noted the birdsong to be "the most melodious wild music I had ever heard, with the most tunable silver sound

A Maori mask carved in wood.

imaginable. They would begin to sing at 1 or 2 in the morning and go on until sunrise." This country too was a natural historian's paradise.

While Banks and Solander botanized, Cook continued his geographical surveys.

CANNIBALS

When Cook, Banks, and some sailors took a boat into a cove one day they found a small group of Maori preparing a meal. Banks's journal tells what they learned:

The family were employed when we came ashore in dressing their provisions, which were a dog who was at that time buried in their oven and near it were many provision baskets. Looking carelessly upon one of these we by accident observed 2 bones, pretty clean picked, which as appeared upon examination were undoubtedly human bones. Tho we had from the first of our arrival upon the coast constantly heard the Indians acknowledge the custom of eating their enemies we had never before had a proof of it, but this amounted almost to demonstration: the bones were clearly human, upon them were evident marks of their having been dressed on the fire, the meat was not entirely picked off from them and on the grisly ends which were gnawed were evident marks of teeth, and these were accidentally found in a provision basket. On asking the people what bones are these? They answered, The bones of a man.—And have you eaten the flesh?—Yes.—Have you none of it left?—No.—Why did you not eat the woman who we saw today in the water?— She was our relation.—And who then is it that you do

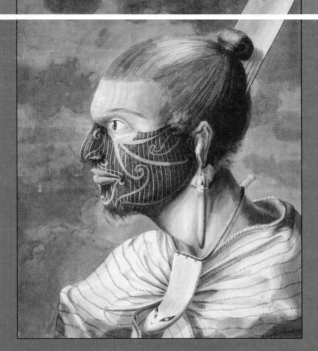

A New Zealander with facial tattooing, drawn by Sidney Parkinson.

eat?—Those who are killed in war. – And who was the man whose bones these are?—5 days ago a boat of our enemies came into this bay and of them we killed 7, of whom the owner of these bones was one.—The horror that appeared in the countenances of the seamen on hearing this discourse which was immediately translated for the good of the company is better conceived than described.

Later, on Cook's second voyage in the Pacific, a quarrel seems to have broken out between a group of sailors on shore and some Maori. Ten of Cook's men were killed and devoured. This was the only example of violence toward the British at the hands of the New Zealanders.

He completed his chart of the New Zealand coastline—2,400 miles (1,488 kilometers)— in under three months. The *Endeavour* sailed away with four hundred new plants, and journals containing a huge amount of new information about places and people.

Next stop would be Australia, where Cook meant to survey the whole eastern coast.

Captain Cook's Voyages

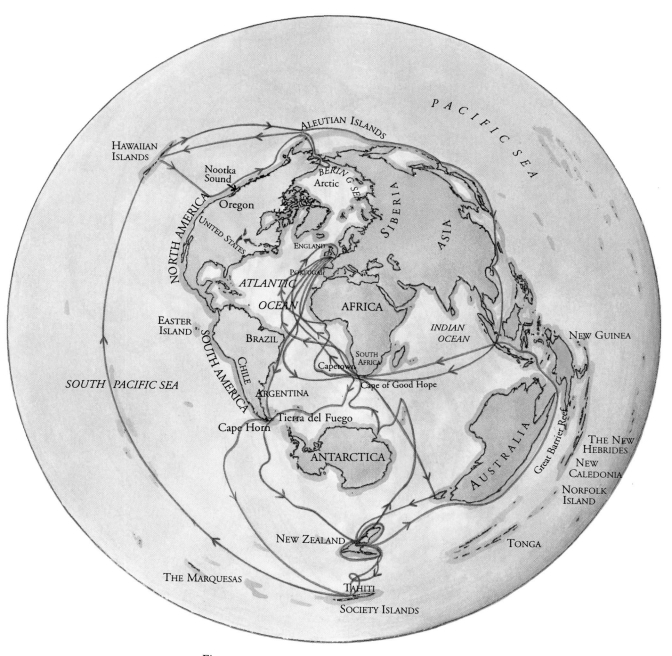

First voyage: 1768-1771
Second voyage: 1772-1775
Third voyage: 1776-1780

SIX

Australia:
A New Continent

In late April 1770 the *Endeavour* anchored in a wide bay in Australia. There were some people on the beach, and others in bark canoes, fishing. The *Endeavour* was the largest structure they had ever seen, so huge and complex they were astounded. Cook sent young Isaac Smith ashore first, then followed with others. "The seal of distance and space that had protected the east coast of Australia since the Pleistocene epoch was broken," wrote the Australian historian Robert Hughes. "The colonization of the last continent had begun."

During the short time Cook stayed he had little contact with the natives. But "it sealed the doom of the Aborigine," Hughes wrote. In 1788 the British would establish a convict colony here whose colonists would soon overcome the Aborigines.

Cook sailed north to begin charting the two thousand miles

A drawing of Australians on what would be called
King George's Sound.

(1,240 kilometers) of the continent's eastern coast. It would take him four months to complete the work. The Spanish had been the first Europeans to see Australia, in 1606. The Dutch came next, in 1616. But they touched only the western and northern parts. The eastern half of Australia was unknown until Cook's arrival. Cook found the land flat and low, the soil sandy. The naturalists collected many new plants. Small groups of people would come by, but their language was so unlike

Polynesian that Tupaia was of no help. The people were short, lean, and dark skinned. They had black hair, and some were bearded. They ignored presents offered to them, not interested in getting anything more than what they already had. And they never stole anything. Are they far happier than we Europeans? Cook wondered.

In June a huge natural obstacle almost ended the voyage: At eleven o'clock one night, the *Endeavour* struck the Great Barrier Reef. Built up by tiny sea animals, this extraordinary coral reef is 1,250 miles (775 kilometers) long and covers 80,000 square miles (30,888 kilometers). Some 350 species of coral created it over a period of 25 million years.

Europeans knew nothing of it until Cook ran into it. He heard a horrible sound as a coral fang ripped through the bottom of the *Endeavour* and broke off, leaving a big hole. The men threw everything overboard: heavy guns, ballast, casks—fifty tons of equipment and supplies. Even then, at high tide twelve hours later, the ship still would not move. As the tide went down she heeled to starboard and began to take in water. All manned the four pumps in fifteen-minute shifts, but the leak kept gaining. If the ship did not come free into deep water she'd sink straight down. At last, as the tide rose, the *Endeavour* floated, got under sail, and headed for land.

At low tide, inspection proved that—by the greatest good luck—a lump of coral rock had stuck in the hole, stopping the fatal inrush of the sea. It took days to repair the damage. Men sent to forage in the country for food brought back pigeons, plantains, cabbages, and taro, an edible root. Fishing added to their diet. The only game animal spotted on land was a strange, swift, mouse-colored animal with a long tail, jumping like a deer. Banks shot two: they were kangaroos. The discovery of the animal provided a change in their diet and a contribution to the world's knowledge of wildlife.

More native people appeared at coastal stops, but never many, for the population was small. The Aborigines had been living in Australia

A watercolor of kangaroos, one of the many animals
new to Cook's men.

for at least 30,000 years, having migrated by sea from Southeast Asia.
They were always shy and nervous, startled by this invasion of aliens.

They were more primitive in their way of life than the Tahitians or
New Zealanders. They went naked, painted their bodies in curious
designs, did not farm the land and lived on fish and shellfish. Their
houses and canoes were small and crudely built. "The most wretched
set I ever beheld," noted one man.

With only three months' provisions left, Cook decided it was time to
head home, even though some of the coast was still unexplored. During

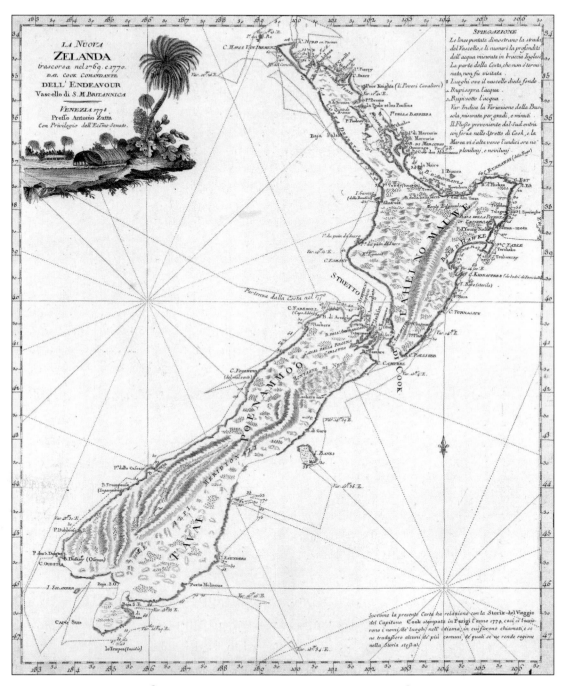

A map of New Zealand, apparently drawn from data
supplied by Captain Cook.

that passage Banks found the bird and sea life very rich. They caught two sharks—a welcome change in diet. Along the way they stopped at islands appearing on no chart, for the Dutch, the Portuguese, and the Spanish were secretive about their holdings in the East Indies. On October 11, 1770, they reached Batavia, headquarters of the Dutch East India Company.

Newspapers from home! They learned that American colonists were refusing to pay taxes to the Crown and that British regiments were being sent to crush signs of rebellion. While the Endeavour was being repaired in the shipyards, diseases such as malaria, common in Batavia, struck Cook's men. Many died, but Cook, Banks, and others recovered. To replace his losses, Cook recruited nineteen Englishmen glad to sail home.

As the *Endeavour* crossed the Indian Ocean, many of the men were overcome by dysentery. They stopped at Cape Town, where the sails and the rigging were overhauled and the ship painted. Cook was able to get his sick men medical care. Nevertheless, a total of thirty-four died on the way home.

On July 12, 1771, they anchored in England, two years and eleven months after leaving home. The next day Cook reported to the Admiralty and was then reunited with his wife and two elder boys, now seven and eight. His youngest son, Joseph, had died at three months, when his father had scarcely gone. So too his young daughter Elizabeth, just as Cook was nearing home. His grief must have been terrible to bear after his long years away from home.

Cook wrote letters to the families of all those in the ship's company who had died. He had an audience with the king, then met with the Admiralty, to whom he recommended promotions for those men deserving it. Within a month a new voyage was proposed, this time to settle, once and for all, whether or not a Great Southern Continent existed. If it did, Cook was to claim it for king and country.

S E V E N

Into the Antarctic

For his second attempt to determine whether a large temperate continent existed in the southern hemisphere, Cook secured two new Whitby colliers—the *Resolution* and the *Adventure*. Both were well fitted and staffed. His naturalists this time would be Johann Forster, a German scientist, and his brilliant young son George. In addition, an astronomer was assigned to each ship. The new chronometer invented by John Harrison was taken aboard; it would prove very effective in determining longitude.

This time Cook's focus was entirely on answering the ancient question about a Great Southern Continent. To reach that part of the globe required sailing around the earth at the most southern latitude. Instead of entering the Pacific by sailing around Cape Horn, Cook went the other way, down the Atlantic coast of Africa to the Cape of Good

A modern photograph of mountains looming over icebergs
in the antarctic.

Hope, where he stayed a month to replenish supplies. And then into the south polar region. In the antarctic, summer lasts for the four months of November through February, and Cook had to get there before winter set in. His ships headed south from Cape Town on November 22, 1772.

When Cook left the Cape of Good Hope, his ships ran into cold stormy weather almost at once. Brutal gales blew that matched hurricanes in ferocity. On December 10 a lookout spied land. Land? It proved to be an icy mountain, blue in color, shaped like a pyramid, rising three hundred feet (ninety-one meters) above the sea. The ocean beat violently against it. Winds that could reach two hundred miles (124 kilometers) per hour had created sculptural ridges on its surface. Smaller chunks of ice in the sea kept banging against the ships' sides, making a great noise.

Rain, sleet, and snow assailed the ships as the temperature dropped below freezing. Ice coated ropes and sails, and thick fog made movement dangerous. Yet when they saw seals and many kinds of birds, Cook pushed farther south, for he felt these creatures would not travel far from land.

A few days later the ships edged up to a huge wall of ice. They did not realize how huge. In one part of the antarctic, the ice sheet extends over an area the size of Texas and Colorado together. Get around it? Impossible. Cook turned east, trying to sail along the edge of the ice to an opening where he could head south again.

But only ten miles on, they were nearly encircled by solid ice. What if they were trapped in the ice? And the ships and men crushed to death as the ice closed in? Cook wisely ordered the ships to sail north to get free of the ice, head east for a while, then try a southern turn once more.

On December 12 master's mate Charles Clerke reported, "Passed an ice island as high as the body of St. Paul's church." On December 16 he wrote, "The fog so very thick we can scarcely see the length of the quarterdeck." It was so bitterly cold that nearly all the stock they had brought from Cape Town—pigs, sheep, chickens—died.

On Christmas day they were still trying to sail around the ice pack. Cook loosened discipline and let the men celebrate the holiday by gulping grog and staging boxing matches. New Year's Day came on. Still no sight of land. Ice, only ice.

When a rare break in weather came, the astronomers calculated longitude in the traditional way, and then by taking readings with the new chronometer. They proved the chronometer worked better than the old method—a vital discovery for navigation.

When Cook spied a break in the ice he had the ships sail south again. The land, where was the land? On January 17, 1773, they crossed the Antarctic Circle. They were the first people ever to sail that far south. The very next day they were hemmed in by pack ice. Ahead they counted thirty-eight huge icebergs, and beyond those, an endless mass of solid field ice.

They were in a seascape so fantastic that no one back home in temperate Europe would believe it. In his journal, Cook noted that the antarctic "exhibits a view which . . . at once fills the mind with admiration and horror, the first is occasioned by the beautifulness of the picture and the latter by the danger attending it."

We know now what Cook didn't know then and was trying to find out. Antarctica *is* a continent, the fifth-largest of all seven continents. It has no set boundaries. Its edges are the South Atlantic, the Indian and the South Pacific oceans. It is twice the size of Australia. But useful to anyone? The ice sheet Cook edged into covers 98 percent of the continent. The other 2 percent is barren rock.

Once upon a time—200 million years ago—Antarctica was joined to South America, Africa, India, and Australia; they were one huge continent. Geologic changes split them apart. The ice sheet Cook gazed at in wonder was at least 20 million years old. About 90 percent of the world's ice and 80 percent of its fresh water are contained in the continent.

Cook's men saw high peaks, part of a mountain range about three miles high. The ice that held back his ships averages seven thousand feet in depth. At its thickest place it is about 16,000 feet (4,900 meters) deep. There is so much ice here that if it were to melt, sea levels would rise some 200 feet (60 meters) worldwide, drowning many parts of the earth.

In March 1773 Cook gave up the search for land and sailed north. The two ships lost sight of each other, but in expectation of separation, they had arranged to rendezvous in New Zealand so that is where they headed.

Several sailors were suffering from frostbite of the hands and feet. (The temperature in the antarctic can fall well below -100° F (-80° C). Despite all Cook's precautions against scurvy, after such a long and unbroken time at sea, symptoms of the disease had begun to appear. A short rest in a safe harbor would do everyone good.

In New Zealand they reunited with their sister ship. They stayed a while, visited Tahiti again, and then Cook, in the *Resolution*, made another try at the antarctic. In late November 1773 Cook and his crew sailed southeast from New Zealand. They saw only icebergs, nothing of land. Waves crashed over the deck, water seeped into every nook and cranny, men shivered in the cold sleet and damp snow. Every now and then terrifying huge icebergs slammed into the ship, once nearly capsizing it.

Christmas again, in the antarctic. And again a day of revelry with big swigs of grog to help the men forget their miserable existence. Whales sporting around the ship and penguins lining up like soldiers on the icebergs were brief distractions.

Though his men were depressed and sorely angry with him, Cook would not give up trying to find the supposed continent. They crossed the Antarctic Circle for the second time on January 26, 1774. Mountains of ice reared up on the horizon, ninety-seven of them by Cook's count. He couldn't possibly steer the ship through them, and just ahead was

A lithograph of a ship caught in the ice in Antarctica.

a sheet of ice so massive Cook thought it must reach to the South Pole.

So he gave up. The *Resolution* turned around and sailed directly north to the tropics—much to the men's disappointment. They feared it would be another year before they got home. They were right. Cook took them in a great loop west across the Pacific, then back again. He meant to improve the charts of old discoveries and to find whatever places in the South Pacific might never before have been reached. They touched on or stayed awhile in many places, with Cook making precise charts everywhere: Easter Island, the Marquesas, Tahiti again, Tonga, the New Hebrides, New Caledonia, Norfolk Island, New Zealand,

Tierra del Fuego. Then, on January 3, 1775, Cook began a third sweep of the antarctic, running into the same appalling conditions as before, with just as little result. But negative discovery can be important too. Cook proved there was no land-continent that could be colonized or developed. Land, yes, but only frozen rock deep beneath the enormous sheet of ice.

They headed home now, by way of the Cape of Good Hope. On July 30, 1775, they anchored at Plymouth, England. They had been gone three years and eighteen days. This time Cook had lost only four men, none from scurvy.

What then were the results of Cook's first two Pacific voyages? In the precise details of the charts he brought back, he demonstrated certain truths about the South Pacific: the existence of the great ice barrier of the antarctic; the relationships among Australia, the twin islands of New Zealand, and New Guinea; and the position of many lesser islands. He broke through the veil of myth and fantasy to bring the world the real South Pacific.

What would he do next?

He would search for the slim needle of a Northwest Passage—a waterway long thought to connect the Pacific with the Atlantic across the northern reaches of North America.

EIGHT

A Northwest Passage?

Yes, the British Admiralty had still another assignment for James Cook—a question that for centuries had called for an answer. Was there really a Northwest Passage? Could a ship sail from the Atlantic to the Pacific or from the Pacific to the Atlantic, across North America? European explorers had tried to find such a passage ever since the late 1500s. Britain's paramount concern was to find a protected route to the riches of Asia without crossing seas controlled by the Spanish and Portuguese and without paying tribute to middlemen on land routes through the Middle East.

Cook's stubborn persistence in penetrating the myths of the South Pacific made the Royal Society decide this was the man for the job. So scarcely a year after his return from the second voyage, Cook would be off again.

Prince William Sound, east of present-day Anchorage, Alaska, where Cook's damaged ship, the <u>Resolution</u>, was repaired. Here, the crew traded with the Eskimos.

But first, he was reunited with his wife and family. Only two of his five children were alive, James (eleven) and Nathaniel (ten), both already headed for careers at sea. Another son joined the family when Hugh was born in May 1776. Cook made his reports to the Admiralty and to the Royal Society, which honored him by election to its distinguished membership. He contributed to its journal an important scientific paper on protecting the health of seamen.

The greatest British artists of his time painted portraits of Cook, and he was welcomed into the clubs of intellectuals. He edited his journal of the voyage to prepare it for publication. This seven-hundred-page work, with charts and illustrations, was itself an historic event, but it did not appear until May 1777, when Cook was again at sea.

Surely Cook had done enough for Britain and for science. The

One of Britain's leading painters of the time, Sir Nathaniel Dance, did this portrait of Captain Cook in May 1776. It is believed to be his best likeness.

government recognized Cook's achievements by providing him with a pension, an annual salary, living quarters, and all expenses. While he accepted the honor, he confessed he wasn't sure he'd like a life of ease in retirement. He made clear that he was always ready to carry out any duty asked of him. When the prospect of a third voyage arose, he eagerly agreed to lead it.

Why? Perhaps this time he felt reasonably confident he'd succeed. Besides, the British Parliament had offered a £20,000 reward for the discoverer of a Northwest Passage.

Cook built upon the experiences of his other voyages in planning the third. The *Resolution* was refitted for the new voyage, and another Whitby collier, the *Discovery*, would join it a little later. He tried to sign on as many of the same officers and crew as he could—thus training another generation of explorers.

They sailed from England on June 25, 1776. It was eight days after the American colonies had broken with Britain by adopting Thomas Jefferson's Declaration of Independence. Both powers in that conflict issued proclamations ordering their warships not to interfere with Captain Cook on this third voyage because of its scientific value to all nations.

Cook planned to search for a Northwest Passage from the Pacific side. The ships headed east around the Cape of Good Hope, across the Indian Ocean to New Zealand, and then on to Tahiti.

In the Tongan islands, in the spring of 1777, the first signs of a change in Cook's personality began to show. The natives—like the Tahitians—continued to steal from the British. In fact, the episodes became more and more frequent. People stole anything left lying loose about the ships, from pewter basins to muskets. When threats drove away the thieves, they climbed trees and flung stones and coconuts at Cook's men. Only when Cook seized their canoes, and some chiefs too, was stolen property returned.

Yet as the thieving went on, Cook's anger mounted, and he lost his self-control. He flogged offenders mercilessly and with a knife slashed crosses on their arms. It shocked his officers and men to see this new side of the humane leader they had respected and admired.

Some medical scientists now suggest that Cook may have been suffering from a parasitic infection of the intestine. Its symptoms include prolonged ill health, fatigue, loss of initiative, depression, and change of personality.

The ships set sail, roaming the Pacific for about eighteen months, until in late January 1778 Cook's men sighted strange new lands. They turned out to be the Hawaiian islands, the northernmost reach of Polynesia. The Hawaiian people welcomed these Europeans, the first ever to visit them. Cook's men found their customs and language were like those of the other Polynesians they had come to know. The Hawaiians had achieved a high level of skill in agriculture and fishing. They had developed aquaculture farms that produced thousands of tons of fish each year. And they farmed the land just as expertly.

Here too Cook laid down strict rules about intimate contact with women. But as before, the men did as they liked. They transmitted venereal disease to the unsuspecting Hawaiians. Cook threatened and punished, yet to no avail. Even his officers disobeyed him. Nor did the Hawaiian women help, for they eagerly sought the attentions of the visitors. Cook punished his men violently, giving way to explosive outbursts of rage.

Nevertheless, trading continued, each side giving and taking what was wanted or needed. On February 2, Cook's ships left Hawaii, sailing northeast. On March 7 they reached the coast of North America, at what is now northern Oregon. Snow-covered mountains in the distance contrasted sharply with the tropical islands. Coasting north they saw that what Spanish explorers had mapped as a strait across the continent was only a river. A week later they anchored at Nootka Sound, not realizing it was on the west coast of huge Vancouver Island (as it was later named for George Vancouver, a veteran of Cook's first voyage). Here they encountered the Nootka Indians, a people quite different from the Polynesians in appearance, customs, language, and arts. Cook hoped to restock food, but this was spring, a time of scarcity, and he got little. The Nootka already had some iron tools, and they wanted more iron. In exchange they offered fishhooks, carved masks of human faces and animal heads, and animal skins.

For just one nail a sailor could be given the finest sea otter fur. Cook noted that this fur was finer and softer than any others he knew of. He predicted, "the discovery of this part of the continent of North

The Hawaiians depicted their gods by carving such wooden figures as these.

A village scene on the west coast of Vancouver Island—a 1778 watercolor by John Webber, an artist on Captain Cook's third voyage.

America . . . where so valuable an article of commerce may be met with, cannot be a matter of indifference." Barely was his expedition over when fur traders arrived, buying so many sea otter skins to sell on the Chinese market that the Indians, in their eagerness to acquire foreign goods, hunted the animal nearly to extinction.

The Nootka showed little interest in the English beyond trading. Cook found that the tribes held slaves, apparently a privilege reserved for the chiefs, for the commoners had none. He stayed four weeks, and when his carpenters had finished repairs to his ships, he continued north. He tried following Russian charts of this region, but found they had little bearing on reality.

Here and there along the coast they saw what might be passages across the continent, but all proved to be false. They followed the coast of the Alaska Peninsula, which points south in the Pacific, then breaks up into the thousand-mile-long chain of the Aleutian Islands. The fog became so thick they sometimes could not see a hundred yards ahead.

After a month of coasting along the Aleutians they sailed through a passage between them and entered the Bering Sea. Cook's was the first ship from Europe to reach the Bering Strait, which separates Siberia from Alaska by only fifty-two miles. They had reached the western limit of North America, where the Bering Sea joins with the Arctic Sea. A great gale swept them across the strait to Siberia. On shore for just a day, they were greeted warmly by the Chukchi people, who were fur hunters.

The men found that the native peoples they encountered on both sides of the Bering Sea spoke nearly the same language. They saw polar bears, bowhead and narwhal whales, arctic foxes, ringed seals, ivory gulls, and snowy owls. In Cook's unrelenting hunt for fresh food to prevent scurvy, he had the men kill some huge walruses squatting on the ice flows. The cook turned their meat into fried steaks. But it tasted so disgusting the men refused to eat it. Furious, Cook banned all other food but ship's biscuit unless they ate walrus. It came close to mutiny before he gave in to the men.

The naturalists delighted in the variety of birds. They ranged from tiny hummingbirds to mallards, gulls, geese, bald eagles, and giant albatrosses. At some arctic rookeries, birds congregated in tens and even hundreds of thousands to nest and feed during the short summer—a remote paradise for bird-watchers.

It was August now, way beyond their deadline for arctic sailing. Yet Cook pushed north, through thick fogs and wild rainstorms. They clung to visible coastline when they could until, on August 17, what appeared to be an extraordinarily white sky ahead turned out to be an impenetrable mass of ice. Twelve feet high, it stretched from horizon to horizon.

The arctic regions cover all the lands north of the Arctic Circle. They embrace the northern parts of Asia, Europe, and North America, as well

An albatross, as depicted by Gustave Doré. This was one of the great variety of birds Cook's men observed in the arctic.

as the Arctic Ocean and its islands. The Arctic Ocean is the fourth largest in the world, with an area of some 5.5 million square miles (2.1 million square kilometers). That is about 1.5 times the size of the continental United States. Most of the arctic's land is covered by a drifting polar ice cap. In the nightless summer, the ice pack is surrounded by open seas. During the dayless winter, the pack more than doubles in size.

A Northwest Passage?

All told, Cook's ships spent nearly four months in this northern region, with Cook reluctant to give up on the quest for a Northwest Passage. By October, though, perilously close to being trapped in a mass of field ice (as in Antarctica), he realized he could go no farther. He would head south, spend the winter improving his charts, and return to the arctic for one more try the following summer.

NINE

We Had Lost a father

In late October 1778 Cook turned south. On November 26 his ships were back in the Hawaiian islands. They sailed along the coasts, trading with people as they went, exchanging axes, knives, chisels, and adzes for fruit, vegetables, and pigs. On January 17, 1779, they sighted a big bay suitable for anchorage—Kealakekua. They entered the bay and a thousand canoes circled the two ships, eager for trade. So many men and women of all ages clambered over the rails that one ship almost capsized. It was a mass boarding close to hysteria. There was wholesale theft, with swimmers even tearing nails out of the ships' sheathing. Not until two chiefs came aboard and forced their people off was order restored.

It was soon clear that Cook was regarded here as a god. A priest knelt before him, presented him with a pig and two coconuts, then

William Hodges, ship's artist on the *Resolution*, captures the weariness of Captain Cook at the end of the second voyage

draped a red cloak over his shoulders. The chiefs insisted he go ashore for a ceremony, which turned into a drunken feast. A few days later, the king of Hawaii himself, with a flotilla of great canoes, arrived to greet Cook.

When Cook's ships sailed out of the bay on February 4, 1779, countless canoes trailed them in an emotional farewell. But suddenly a great storm blew up, shattering the foremast of the *Resolution* and reopening an old leak in the ship. They needed to return to Kealakekua to make repairs.

It puzzled them that they were not greeted warmly this time. The carpenters began repairs on the ships, expecting it might take two weeks. As they started, thieves stole some of their tools. When one was caught, he was given forty lashes. Despite Cook's protests to the chiefs, the thefts continued. Then while some of his men were collecting fresh water, they were stoned. The assaults enraged Cook, who ordered his men to fire their muskets from now on if they came upon thieves.

This was only the beginning of several violent incidents, in which people on both sides became victims. The natives lost four chiefs and thirteen others.

On February 14, one of Cook's small boats was stolen. When Cook went ashore to protest, a crowd of warriors gathered around, armed with spears, clubs, and daggers. They threw stones at Cook and his men. Seeing a man begin to hurl a spear at him, Cook shot and killed him. The enraged Hawaiians attacked Cook with knives and clubs. As he staggered into the water where his boats lay offshore, the warriors grabbed him and held him under until he drowned. Then they dragged him out, flung his corpse on the rocks, and struck it again and again with clubs and knives.

Many of Cook's men, horrified, cried out for revenge. But calmer heads prevailed. The day after his death, part of Cook's body was returned to his men. His remains were buried in the bay. He was fifty years old when he died.

The two highest-ranking officers under Cook—John Gore and Charles Clerke—took command of the ships. They were determined to continue the search for the Northwest Passage. In July 1779 they reached the Bering Strait. But they too soon ran into that immense ice pack, with no way around or through it. They gave up and headed home by way of the Cape of Good Hope.

Both ships anchored in England on October 4, 1780. They had been gone four years, two months, and twenty-two days.

Other explorers would soon try to find a Northwest Passage. But by 1820 no one believed any longer that such a route would make commercial sense. The arctic ice was too variable, the latitude too high,

The fight between Captain Cook's men and the Hawaiians on
February 14, 1779, that led to the death of the explorer,
as envisioned by the painter J. Clevely.

the season too short. Still, adventurous souls kept trying, urged on by
the desire to gather more geographic and scientific knowledge. It was
Roald Amundsen, a Norwegian polar explorer, who in 1903 to 1906
would be the first to complete the northern crossing in a single ship.

Cook's men, on all his voyages, had both feared and loved him.
"We all felt we lost a father," one man said. "The spirit of discovery, the
decision, the indomitable courage, were gone." And another remembered, "We used to look up to him as our good genius, our safe conductor
and as a kind of superior being." Many felt how ironic it was that he had
been so popular with all of the Polynesian islanders, who respected his
fair way of dealing with them, yet they had become his killers.

Cook's self-assurance, his boundless confidence in his own judgment, his readiness to press his crew to any limit to achieve their goals—these were what had made his great achievements possible. On this third and last voyage, however, his fatigue, his illness, and his growing sense that this time he would not achieve the goal, somehow combined to explode in the anger that led to his death.

Discovery, whether by Cook or any other explorer, is a mutual process. The people Cook "discovered" were exploring too, trying to find out who these foreigners were who landed on their shores, what they wanted, what their customs and habits and nature were. Early on, Cook had begun to see some of the negative effects of his voyages on the Pacific peoples. But as a scientific investigator, discovery of the new and significant was his highest goal.

Some hold that Cook should be remembered not so much for finding new lands as for his unsurpassed charting of coastlines and his careful mapping of whole continents. His voyages expanded as never before the world's knowledge of geography. They brought a great amount of natural science to the world. Thousands of new plant and animal species were described. Astronomy and navigation were advanced.

Many single out what Cook did to prevent scurvy. His proof that the frighteningly high rate of death on long voyages could be reduced to nearly zero was of great and lasting importance worldwide.

It took four years for the Admiralty's official account of the voyage, based largely upon Cook's journals as well as those of others, to be published. It appeared in 1784 in three volumes illustrated by engravings and charts. It proved immensely popular. Cheaper and smaller editions reached an even wider readership. Mrs. Cook received half the royalties and a pension. She died in 1835, at the age of ninety-three. Her grief at the news of her husband's death can only be imagined. Yet she was a sailor's wife, who understood the risks of her husband's way of life. It is

A
NEW VOYAGE,
ROUND THE WORLD,

IN THE YEARS
1768, 1769, 1770, AND 1771;

Undertaken by Order of his prefent Majefty,

PERFORMED BY,

CAPTAIN JAMES COOK,

IN THE SHIP ENDEAVOUR,

Drawn up from his own Journal, and from the Papers of

JOSEPH BANKS, Esq. F. R. S.

And publifhed by the fpecial Direction of
the Right Honourable the
LORDS OF THE ADMIRALTY.

By JOHN HAWKESWORTH, L. L. D.
And late Director of the Eaft-India Company.

IN TWO VOLUMES:
With Cutts and a Map of the whole Navigation.

VOL. I.

NEW-YORK:

Printed for WILLIAM AIKMAN, Bookfeller and Stationer,
at Annapolis, 1774.

painful to realize that in their seventeen years of marriage they had rarely been together for more than a few months at a time—taken all together, just four years.

Public interest in Cook has continued to this day, with his life celebrated in biographies, plays, ballads, novels, children's stories—and monuments, over two hundred in all!

Title page of presumed report on Cook's first voyage, produced by the journalist John Hawkesworth. It was done without the captain's cooperation and was full of errors, infuriating Cook.

CAPTAIN COOK AND HIS TIMES

1728 James Cook born

1755 Joins Royal Navy

1756 Seven Years' War breaks out

1763 Marries Elizabeth Batts

1768 Commands an expedition to the Pacific to observe the Transit of Venus

1769 Anchors in Tahiti

1770 Anchors at Botany Bay, Australia and the *Endeavor* strikes the Great Coral Reef

1773 Crosses Antarctic Circle for the first time

1774 Crosses Antarctic Circle for the second time

1775 Embarks on last antarctic sweep. Pronounced post-captain, his commission personally handed to him by George III

1778 First Hawaiian islands sighted. Anchors at Nootka Sound, Vancouver Island

1779 Cook is killed

Further Research

Books

Blumberg, Rhoda. *The Remarkable Voyages of Captain Cook*. New York, New York: Bradbury, S & S, 1991

Hancy, David. *Captain James Cook & the Explorers of the Pacific*. Mahwah, New Jersey: Troll Communications, 1979.

Harley, Ruth. *Captain James Cook*. Mahway, New Jersey: Troll Communications, 1979.

Langley, Andrew. *Exploring the Pacific: The Explorations of Captain Cook (Great Explorers series)*. Broomall, Pennsylvania: Chelsea House, 1993

Middleton, Haydn. *Captain Cook: The Great Ocean Explorer (What's Their Story? series)* New York, New York: Oxford University Press, 1998.

Steffof, Rebecca. *Scientific Explorers: Travels in Search of Knowledge (Extraordinary Explorers series)*. New York, New York: Oxford University Press 1993.

Sylvester, David W. *Captain Cook & the Pacific (Then & There series)*. White Plains, New York: Longman, 1971

Websites:

Captain James Cook, The World's Explorer
    http://members.tripod.com/~cuculus/cook/html

Captain James Cook
    http://www.geocities.com/TheTropics/7557/

Captain James Cook of Whitby
    http://www.queensland.co.uk/james.html

Captain James Cook and the Endeavor
    http://albany.virtualave.net/captain_cook.htm

BIBLIOGRAPHY

Beaglehole, J. C. *The Life of Captain James Cook.* Stanford, CA: Stanford University Press, 1974.

Boorstin, Daniel. *The Discoverers.* New York: Vintage, 1985.

Constance, Arthur. *The Impenetrable Sea.* New York: Citadel Press, 1958.

Cuppage, Francis E. *James Cook and the Conquest of Scurvy.* Westport, CT: Greenwood Press, 1994.

Delgado, James. *Across the Top of the World.* New York, NY: Checkmark Books, 1999.

Hobsbawm, E. J. *The Age of Revolution: 1789 to 1848.* New York: Mentor, 1962.

Hough, Richard. *Captain James Cook.* New York: W.W. Norton & Co., 1995.

Hughes, Robert. *The Fatal Shore.* New York: Vintage, 1988.

Lopez, Barry. *Arctic Dreams: Imagination and Desire in a Northern Landscape.* New York: Bantam, 1996.

Morison, Samuel Eliot. *The Great Explorers.* New York: Oxford University Press, 1978.

O'Brian, Patrick. *Joseph Banks: A Life.* Chicago: University of Chicago Press, 1997.

Plumb, J. H. *England in the Eighteenth Century.* New York: Penguin, 1950.

Price, A. Grenfell, ed. *The Explorations of Captain James Cook in the Pacific: As Told by Selections of His Own Journals, 1768 to 1779.* New York: Dover, 1971.

Pyne, Stephen J. *The Ice: A Journey to Antarctica.* Seattle: University of Washington Press, 1998.

Savours, Ann. *The Search for the North West Passage.* New York: St. Martin's Press, 1999.

Sobel, Dava. *Longitude.* New York: Walker, 1995

Bibliography

Stannard, David E. *Before the Horror: The Population of Hawaii on the Eve of Western Contact*. Honolulu: University of Hawaii Press, 1989.

Thomas, Nicholas, and Mark Adams. *Cook's Sites: Revisiting History*. Denedin, NZ:University of Otago Press, 1999.

Withey, Lynne. *Voyages of Discovery: Captain Cook and the Exploration of the Pacific*. Berkeley: University of California Press, 1987.

INDEX

Page numbers for illustrations are in boldface.

maps
  Captain Cook's voyages, 43
  New Zealand, 48

Adventure, 50, 54
Africa, 50–52
Alaska, 63–64
albatrosses, 31
Aleutian Islands, 64
American colonies, 18–20, **20**, 49, 60
Amundsen, Roald, 70
animals, 17, 27, 28, 33, 38–39, 52, 71
  Arctic, 64
  See also albatrosses; kangaroos; penguins; sharks; whales
Antarctica, **51**, 52–54, 75
anthropology, 27, 33
Arctic, 64–65, 69–70
artists
  portrait painters, 58, 59, 68
  on voyages, 27, 28, 33, 63
astronomy, 21, 22, 27, 32, 34
Atlantic Ocean, 11, 28, 31, 50–52
Australia, 44–49, **45**, 75

Banks, Sir Joseph, 28, **29**, 31, 32, 33, 38–39, 46
Batavia, 49
Batts, Elizabeth (wife), 20–21, 26, 71–73
Bering Strait, 64, 69
biographers, 11, 21

Canada, 18–20

cannibalism, 38, 40
Cape Horn, 32
Cape of Good Hope, 50–52, 56, 60, 69
Capetown, 49
captives, 38
ceremonies, 30
chronometer, 50, 53
Clerke, Charles, 52, 69
coal, 10
colliers. See ships
Colville, Lord, 20
Cook, James
  achievements, 30–31, 58, 71–72
  appearance, **17**, 20–21, **59**, **68**
  birth, 7
  children, 21, 49
  death, 69, **70**, 75
  education, 7–8, 10–12, 18–19
  honors and rewards, 58–60
  personality, 8–9, 60–61, 64, 70–71
  in Royal Navy, 16–20, **17**
  and the sea, 9
  wife, 20–21, 26, 71–73
  youth, 7–13, **8**, 15
crew, 25–28, 34–35, 61, 70
  See also disease; sailors
Cuppage, Francis E., 31

deaths
  of Captain Cook, 69, **70**, 75
  of crew, 28, 30, 32, 41, 49, 56

of native peoples, 34–35, 38
discipline, 27, 35, 53, 60–61, 68–69
Discovery, 60
disease
  of Captain Cook, 61
  of crew, 30–31, 49, 71
  venereal, 34–35, 61
  See scurvy
Drake, Sir Francis, **14**, 15
Dutch East India Company, 49

Easter Island, 55
eclipse, 21
economics, 24
Endeavour, **25**, 25–26, 46
England, 13, 16–18, 24–25, 57
equator, crossing, 30

food, 26, 28, 30–31, 33, 38, 46, 47–49, 64, 67
Forster, George, 50
Forster, Johann, 50
French and Indian War, 18–20, **20**

George III, **23**, 75
Gore, John, 69
Great Coral Reef, 46, 75
Great Southern Continent, 24, 36, 50, 56
guides. *See* Tupaia

Hawaiian Islands, 61, **62**, 67–69, 75
health, of sailors, 58, 71

Index

Holland, Samuel, 18–19
Hughes, Robert, 44

icebergs, **6**, 54–55, **55**
ice cap, Arctic, 64–66, 69–70
Industrial Revolution, 10
instruments, 26, 50

journals, 27, 42, 58, 71–73, **72**

kangaroos, 46, 47
King George's Sound, 45

Lind, James, 30
liquor, 27, 30, 53, 54
London, **13**, 13–14, **20**
longitude, 50, 53

Madeira, 28
Magellan, Ferdinand, 24, 31
malaria, 49
Maoris, 36–41, **37**, **39**, **41**
map making. *See* sea charting; surveying
Marquesas, 55
medical historians, 31
morale, 54

native peoples
  of Australia, 44, **45**
  customs, 27
  exploration impact, 71
  of Hawaii, 61, **62**, 64, 67–69, **70**
  of New Zealand, 36–41, **37**, **39**, **41**
  of Siberia, 64
  of Tahiti, 32–35, **33**
  of Tierra del Fuego, 31
  of Tonga, 60
  of Vancouver Island, 62–63, **63**
naturalists. *See* Banks, Sir Joseph; Forster, George; Forster, Johann; Solander, Daniel
navigation. *See* chronometer; sea charting
New Caledonia, 55
New Guinea, 56
New Hebrides, 55
New Zealand, 36–42, 54, 55–56
Newfoundland, 21
Nootka Sound, 61–62
Norfolk Island, 55
North America, 61–66
Northwest Passage, 57, 60, 61–66, 69–70

Oregon coast, 61–62
ownership, 35, 46

Pacific Ocean, 24, 32, 36, 60
  See also South Pacific
Palliser, Captain Hugh, 18
Parkinson, Sidney, 28, 33, 37
Patagonia, 31
penguins, 31, 54
plants, 27, 28, 42, 45, 71
political power, 24
Polynesia, 32, 34, 61
poverty, 13–14
Prince William Sound, **58**
property, 35, 46
publications, 58, 71–73, **72**

Quakers, 9–10

Resolution, 50, 54, 55, 58, 60
Revolutionary War, 60
Rio de Janeiro, 30
Royal Society, 21, 24, 58

sailors, 11, 15, 16, 58
  See also crew
Sanderson, William, 9
science, 24, 27, 58, 71
scurvy, 30–31, 56, 64, 71
sea charting, 18–20, 21, 24
seaports, 9, **10**
Seven Years War, 18–20, **20**
sharks, 47–49
ships
  for coal, 10, 11, 15
  for voyages, 25, **25**, 50, 60
  for war, 18, **19**
Siberia, 64
Smith, Isaac, 44
Society Islands, 36
Solander, Daniel, 28, 33
South Pacific, 55–56, 60–62
stealing, 35, 46, 60, 64, 68–68
storms, 11, 28, 31, 52, 68
sun, distance from, 21, 22, 34
supplies, 26, 28, 47, 50–52
  See also food; instruments
surveying, 18–19, 21, 26, 33, 39–42, 44–45, **48**, 55–56

Tahiti, 21, 24, 32, 54, 55, 75
  See also native peoples
Tierra del Fuego, 31–32, 56
timeline, 75
Tonga, 55, 60
trade
  and England, 24, 57
  with natives, 35, 38, 61–64
Tupaia, 35, 36, 45

United States. *See* American colonies

Vancouver Island, 62, **63**, 75
Venus, Transit of, 22, 27, 32, 34

Walker, James, 9–10, 15
Walker, Mrs, 7
weather, 30–31, 52–53, 56
  See also storms
Webber, John, 63
Websites, 76
whales, 54, 64